PATCHWORK QUILT DESIGNS
Coloring Book

Carol Schmidt

DOVER PUBLICATIONS, INC.
Mineola, New York

Note

Patchwork quilting became popular in America during the eighteenth century. It was a great way to use up leftover scraps of material, and pieces of fabric from special occasions like weddings and baptisms were often included in a quilt to create a cherished family heirloom. The "quilting circle" or "bee" was a social event where women went for good conversation and to work on their quilts. These sentimental keepsakes were passed from generation to generation and were often mentioned in the family will. In this coloring book you will find some of the most common "traditional" patchwork quilt patterns including Log Cabin, Star of Bethlehem, and Tumbling Blocks. You can color the patterns with crayon, felt-tip pen, or pencil. If you want to create an interesting effect, try mixing your coloring methods.

Bibliographical Note

Patchwork Quilt Designs Coloring Book, first published by Dover Publications, Inc., in 2014, contains all the plates from *Traditional Patchwork Quilt Designs,* originally published by Dover in 2007.

International Standard Book Number
ISBN-13: 978-0-486-78031-3
ISBN-10: 0-486-78031-7

Manufactured in the United States by Courier Corporation
78031701   2014
www.doverpublications.com

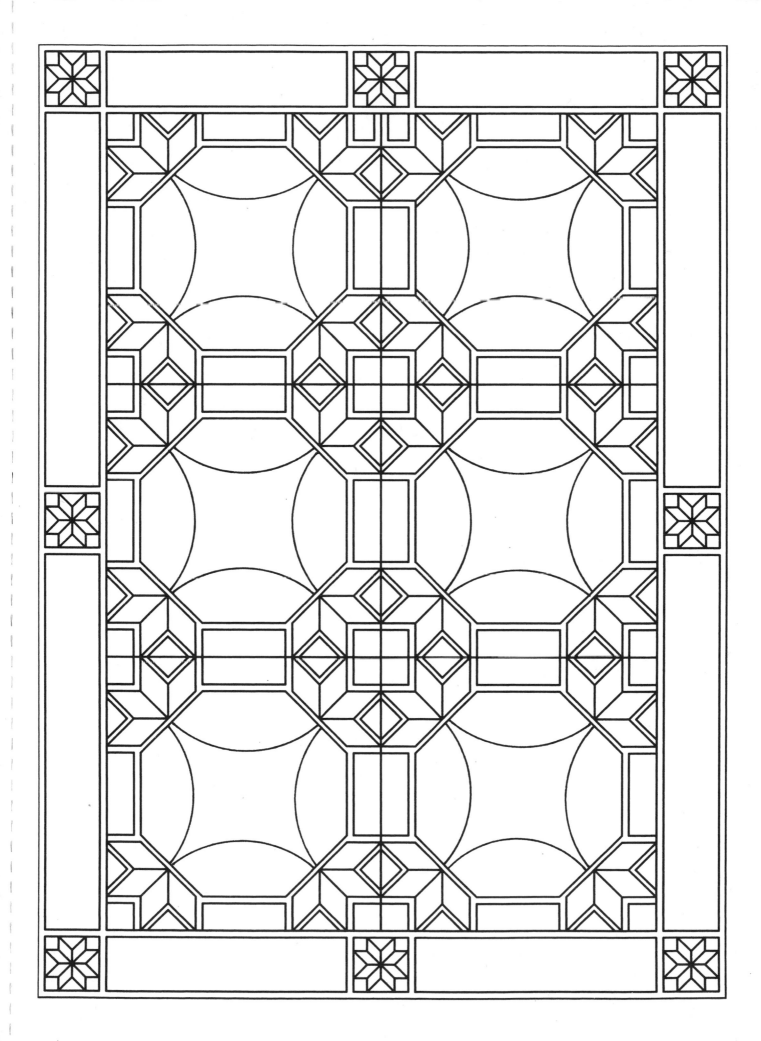

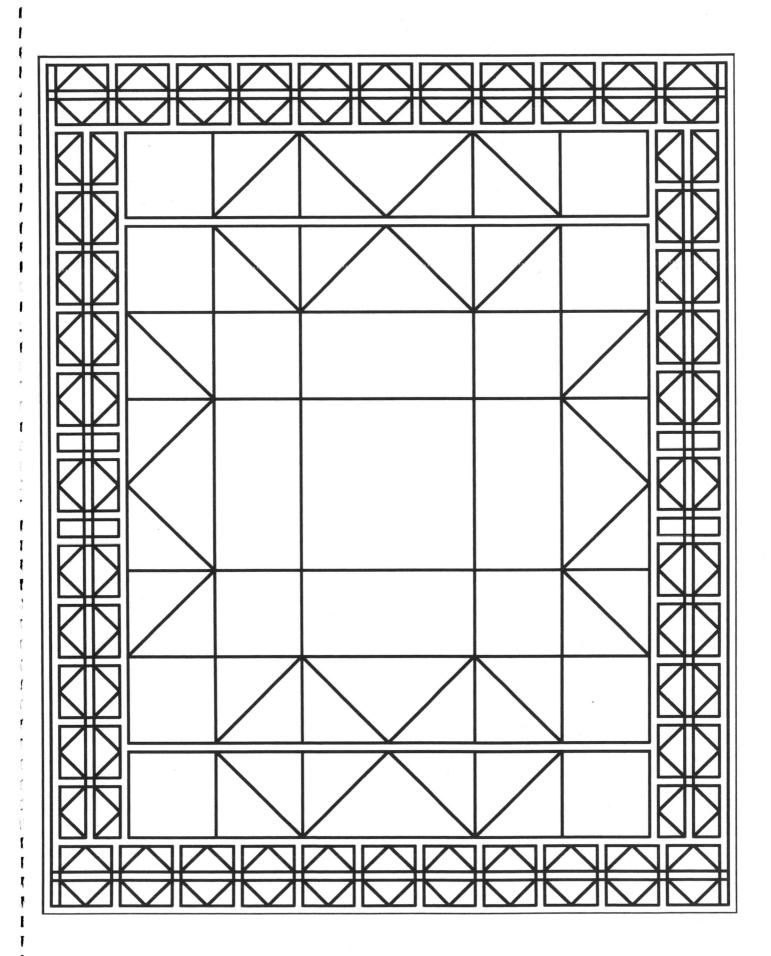

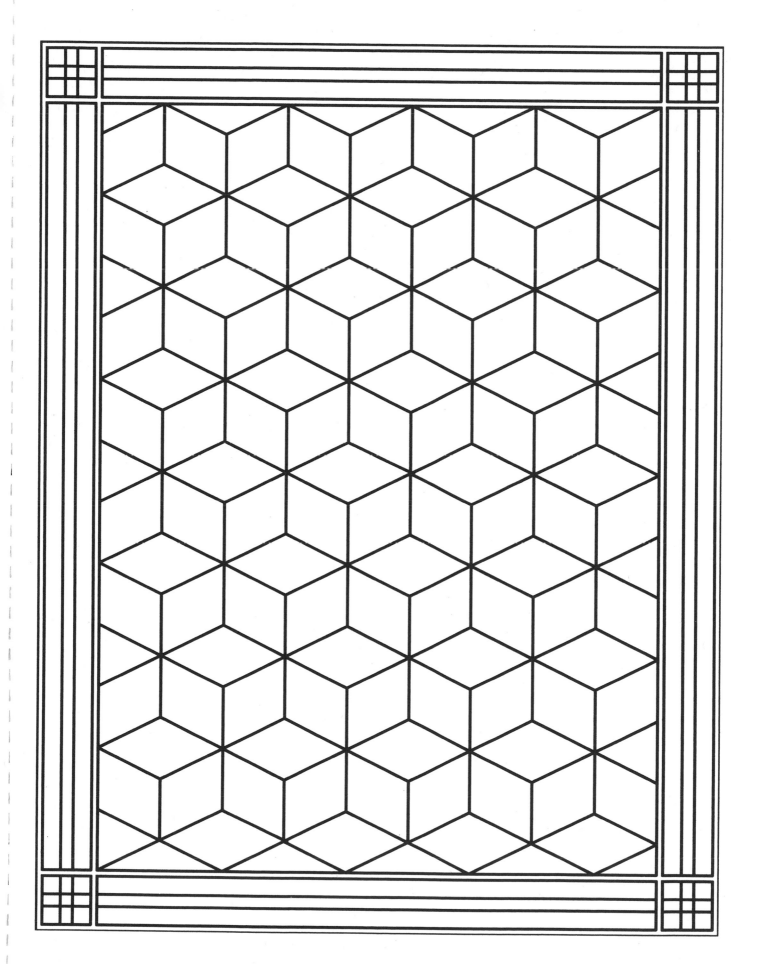